Published by Paperview Europe Ltd.

Printed and bound
by Indice S.L.

CHILDREN
OF THE WORLD

How Your Encyclopedia Works

👉 Mickey, Minnie, Donald, Daisy, Goofy and Pluto are ready to take you on an adventure ride through the world of learning. Discover the secrets of science, nature, our world, the past and much more. Climb aboard and enjoy the ride.

Look here for a general summary of the theme

Labels tell you what's happening in the pictures

Mickey's ears lead you to one of the main topics

The pictures by themselves can tell you a lot, even before you read a word

Watch out for special pages where Mickey takes a close look at some key ideas

Mickey's page numbers help you look things up. Don't forget there's a glossary and index at the back of each book

Goofy and his friends know how to give you a chuckle on every topic

Mickey points you to more information in other books in your *Encyclopedia*

The Solar System

👉 The Solar System is the name given to our Sun and its family of planets. It also includes the planets' moons, millions of pieces of rock called asteroids and meteoroids, and frozen lumps of dust and gas called comets. Everything else you can see in the sky is outside the Solar System and is far, far away. Every single star is itself a sun, and each may have its own family of planets and moons.

Saturn is surrounded

REPTILES AND AMPHIBIANS

COLOR AND CAMOUFLAGE

Color and Camouflage

Frogs and toads come in nearly every imaginable color, even gold or black. They have a wide range of patterns, from spots and stripes to zigzags.

Color and pattern help frogs and toads survive. Bright colors warn that they may be poisonous. Drab colors camouflage them, or hide them against their background. Many tree frogs are exactly the same green as leaves, while others look like bark. The Asian horned toad has the best camouflage of all. Folds of patchy, brown skin and a flat body make it look like a dead leaf when it lies still on the forest floor.

Folds of brown skin give perfect camouflage

Flat body is hard to see among dead leaves

Asian horned toad

False-eyed frog

Markings look like eyes

For extra protection, bad-smelling liquid oozes out around false eyes

FALSE-EYED FROG
The South American false-eyed frog has large markings on its flanks that look like eyes. These fool some predators into thinking that they are looking at a much larger animal, such as a cat or bird.

Dog sniffing curiously at the toad

Oriental fire-bellied toad defending itself against a dog

Skin oozes a stinging fluid

Strawberry arrow frog

POISON-DART FROGS
Deadly poison oozes from the skin of Central and South American poison-dart frogs. People in the rain forest rub the tips of their arrows and blowpipe darts on the skin of these frogs to collect the poison to use for hunting.

Blue poison-dart frog

Bright colored belly

Green and black back

FIRE-BELLIED TOAD
When cornered by a predator, the Oriental fire-bellied toad of eastern Asia arches its back and rears up on its legs to show its fiery underside. Wise attackers back off, because the toad's skin oozes a stinging, bad-tasting fluid.

Toad rears up on its back legs

FIND OUT MORE
MAMMALS: Camouflage
PLANET EARTH: Forests

16

17

FIND OUT MORE
THE KINGDOM OF MAMMALS: Camouflage
PLANET EARTH: Forests

AMAZING FACTS

★ The Sun is enormous compared to the planets. It is nearly 1,000 times more massive than the giant planet Jupiter.

Your favourite characters present some facts to astound you and your friends

HOW OUR SOLAR SYSTEM WAS FORMED

1 The Solar System formed 4.6 billion years ago. It started at the centre of an enormous swirling cloud of gas and dust.

2 The Sun burst into flames and became a star. Its light and warmth spread throughout the new Solar System.

3 Gas and dust left over from making the Sun clumped together in places. These clumps grew bigger and formed the planets.

4 The planets closest to the Sun are small and made from rock and metal. The larger outer planets are made from gas and liquid.

Numbers lead *you step-by-step through how things happen*

Colourful boxes *zoom in on information*

Pluto was the farthest planet from the Sun until 2006, when it was reclassified as a minor planet

Each planet has its own path, or orbit

Planet orbits

ORBITING THE SUN

No matter how still you try to be, you are always moving. This is because the Earth – and all the other planets – are moving. They are flying through Space around the Sun in looping paths called orbits.

Neptune is a cold, blue planet

Uranus is tipped over on its side

THE "PULL" OF GRAVITY

If you throw a ball into the air, it comes down again. The invisible force that pulls it down to Earth is called gravity. The Earth's gravity holds us down on the ground. The Sun's gravity is strong enough to hold all its planets in their orbits.

Gravity pulls a ball to Earth

FIND OUT MORE
PLANET EARTH: Night and day
THE MARVELS OF SCIENCE: Gravity

Mars is red and dusty

The Solar System

Mickey's helpers test some ideas themselves

Contents

Children of the World

Children's lives are very different from place to place. They may live in city apartments, in jungle villages or on lonely farms. They may travel by bike, camel or canoe. They speak different languages and play different games.

Wherever they are, children learn, work and play in the local ways and share in local customs. But the lessons they are taught and the games they play have a common purpose around the world: preparing them to be tomorrow's grown-ups.

Countries of the World

The world is divided into over 180 countries. Some countries, such as China, are very large. Others, such as Costa Rica, are quite small. Many countries have a big population. This means they have a lot of people living in them. The people of a country have their own languages and customs, or ways of life, which vary all over the world.

Latvian folk dance

MAPPING THE WORLD

From Space, Earth looks like a globe, or ball, covered with blue oceans and large blocks of land called continents. The continents – North America, South America, Europe, Africa, Asia and Australia – are divided up into countries.

Key to Numbered Countries

1 Guatemala	16 Portugal	32 Czech Republic
2 Belize	17 Andorra	33 Austria
3 El Salvador	18 Monaco	34 Slovakia
4 Honduras	19 France	35 Hungary
5 Nicaragua	20 Netherlands	36 Slovenia
6 Costa Rica	21 Belgium	37 Croatia
7 Panama	22 Luxembourg	38 Bosnia Herzegovina
8 Guyana	23 Switzerland	39 Serbia-Montene
9 Surinam	24 Liechtenstein	40 Macedonia
10 French Guiana	25 San Marino	41 Albania
11 Paraguay	26 Italy	42 Greece
12 Uruguay	27 Vatican City	43 Bulgaria
13 Iceland	28 Malta	44 Romania
14 Republic of Ireland	29 Denmark	45 Moldova
15 United Kingdom	30 Germany	
	31 Poland	

ARCTIC OCEAN

SWEDEN
NORWAY
FINLAND
EUROPE
RUSSIA

Saami family from northern Finland

AMAZING FACTS

★ The number of countries changes all the time as some countries join together, or others split up into separate countries.

KAZAKHSTAN
GEORGIA
UZBEKISTAN
TURKMENISTAN
MONGOLIA
ASIA
JAPAN

Korean children in traditional costume

TURKEY
IRAN
AFGHANISTAN
CHINA
SPAIN
ALGERIA
LIBYA
EGYPT
SAUDI ARABIA
IRAQ
PAKISTAN
NEPAL
INDIA
OMAN
MALI
NIGER
CHAD
SUDAN
YEMEN
AFRICA
NIGERIA
ETHIOPIA
SOMALIA
SRI LANKA
MALAYSIA
MALDIVES
GABON
CONGO
KENYA
TANZANIA
SEYCHELLES
INDONESIA
PHILIPPINES
PAPUA NEW GUINEA
PACIFIC ISLANDS
ANGOLA
COMOROS
INDIAN OCEAN
EAST TIMOR
ZAMBIA
MADAGASCAR
MAURITIUS
NAMIBIA
SWAZILAND
SOUTH AFRICA
AUSTRALIA
AUSTRALASIA
NEW ZEALAND

Each country has its own flag

There are hundreds of islands in the Caribbean and Pacific. There are 14 independent countries in the Caribbean, and 8 in the Pacific.

46 Estonia
47 Latvia
48 Lithuania
49 Belarus
50 Ukraine
51 Cyprus
52 Syria
53 Lebanon
54 Israel
55 Jordan
56 Kuwait
57 Bahrain
58 Qatar
59 United Arab Emirates
60 Armenia

61 Azerbaijan
62 Tajikistan
63 Kyrgyzstan
64 Bhutan
65 Bangladesh
66 Myanmar (Burma)
67 Thailand
68 Laos
69 Vietnam
70 Cambodia
71 Singapore
72 Brunei
73 North Korea
74 South Korea
75 Tunisia

76 Morocco
77 Mauritania
78 Senegal
79 Gambia
80 Cape Verde
81 Guinea-Bissau
82 Guinea
83 Sierra Leone
84 Liberia
85 Burkina Faso
86 Ivory Coast
87 Ghana
88 Togo
89 Benin
90 Cameroon
91 Equatorial Guinea

92 São Tomé & Príncipe
93 Central African Republic
94 Eritrea
95 Djibouti
96 Uganda
97 Rwanda
98 Burundi
99 Democratic Republic of Congo
100 Malawi
101 Zimbabwe
102 Mozambique
103 Botswana
104 Lesotho

FIND OUT MORE
ATLAS OF THE WORLD: Maps
PLANET EARTH: Earth in Space

11

China and its Neighbours

China and its neighbours are on the continent of Asia. China's population is so big that one out of every four people in the world lives there. It has 56 different nationalities, or groups of people, so it has many languages and customs. China's neighbours – Mongolia, North Korea and South Korea – share some of China's customs and traditions.

BEND AND STRETCH

Children in a Chinese school do exercises together in the schoolground each morning. The exercises – and the music – are the same in every school in China, and judges give prizes to the best schools.

Teachers have large classes, with up to 60 pupils

Exercises are performed in time to music from a loudspeaker

Red kerchiefs are symbols of the Young Pioneers, a national children's organisation

Exercising in a Chinese school

GOING BY BIKE

Bicycles are a way of life in China. Only a few families own cars, so most people travel by bike. There are over 200 million bikes in China, so the roads can become crowded with cyclists.

Cyclists on the streets of Beijing, China

TRADITIONAL CLOTHES

Many South Koreans live in high-rise apartments in big cities, but they still follow some of the old customs of their country. On special occasions children dress in traditional *hanbok* outfits. *Han* means "Korean" and *bok* means "clothing."

Hanbok is usually made of silk

WRITING WITH A BRUSH

Schoolchildren in China use a brush to practise writing the Chinese language. Chinese uses about 60,000 different picture characters instead of letters. Even young schoolchildren must learn more than 1,000 characters.

AMAZING FACTS

★ Approximately 16 million babies are born in China every year.

★ More children live in China than in any other country in the world.

Brush may be *used for writing*

Ink

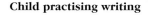

Child practising writing

FIND OUT MORE

ATLAS OF THE WORLD: China
THE WORLD OF ART: Calligraphy

Japan

Japan is a group of islands east of China. Like China, it is part of Asia. Japan is a modern country with many big cities. Japanese children can use the latest computers or ride on some of the fastest trains in the world. But the Japanese people also like to keep alive ancient customs that make their country special. Children learn to join in celebrations that have not changed for hundreds of years.

EARTHQUAKE DRILL

Earthquakes are a constant worry in Japan. Some schoolchildren have regular drills in which they practise what to do in case there is an earthquake. During drills, they may also carry special bags containing emergency supplies.

Children are taught to bend their heads down to keep safe

Dolls are dressed in traditional clothes

CHILDREN'S FESTIVALS

May 5 is *Kodomono-hi,* or Children's Day, and boys fly flags shaped like fish high above the rooftops. *Hina Matsuri,* on March 3, is the day of the doll festival. On this day, girls arrange special dolls in the best room in the house.

Girls arrange dolls in a special order, wishing for good health

Hollow carp flags fill with air on windy festival days

Setting out *Hina Matsuri* dolls

MAD FOR *MANGA*

Many Japanese children enjoy watching colourful cartoons and reading brightly coloured comics called *manga*. *Manga* are about all kinds of subjects, from dinosaurs to superheroes.

Video screen showing *manga* cartoon in Tokyo

Children practising earthquake drill

Padded headgear
to protect children
from falling objects

Girl removing shoes

SOFT SHOE SHUFFLE

When they enter their homes, Japanese families take off their outdoor shoes and leave them by the front door. Inside the house, they wear soft slippers, tabi (socks) or just bare feet.

AMAZING FACTS

★ The Japanese eat more seaweed per person than anyone else in the world. They wrap it around rice or sprinkle it over noodles.

FIND OUT MORE
ATLAS OF THE WORLD: Japan
PLANET EARTH: Earthquakes

Living in the City

Half the people in the world live in cities. A lot of city centres are modern and wealthy with banks, tall office buildings and hospitals. They also have museums, parks and plenty of movie theaters, stores and restaurants.

However, big cities have problems, too. Many cities are overcrowded. Some people do not have their own homes and live in poverty on the streets. Cities may also be polluted with factory smoke and traffic fumes.

Central Park in New York, U.S.

CITY PARKS

Many cities have squares, gardens, or parks with grassy areas, quiet and shady places and water fountains. Some large parks even have lakes. People visit parks to relax or to play games.

Shoppers in the Lotte shopping mall in Seoul, South Korea

SHOPPING MALLS

Cities are the best places to find a good choice of stores and restaurants. Many are grouped together in shopping malls. Some big shopping malls contain amusement centres, movie theatres and even ice-skating rinks.

Cities have a wide range of shops

BUSY STREETS

Cars, buses and streetcars fill most city streets. Traffic fumes can cause health problems, and some cities limit the number of cars on the roads at one time.

Washing is sometimes dried on long poles outside apartment windows

Office building

City trains often travel on rails built above street level

食事処太湖
SEAFOOD RESTAURANT
海鮮料理太湖月
城北電器
Tomorrow Co.
Bakery YAMAMOTO
三省堂書店
高田果物
西口 マーケット
西村 三木宝石

Traffic moves slowly on the busy main streets of most large cities

Strong balconies protect the people who live in high-rise apartments

Busy city streets in Tokyo, Japan

HIGH-RISE LIVING

With buildings and roads covering nearly all the land in a city, there is only one way to build – up! High-rise office and apartment buildings are many stories tall.

FIND OUT MORE
GREAT INVENTIONS: Skyscrapers
TRANSPORT: Cars

17

Cultural Diversity

Big cities are multi-cultural environments. This means that people come from all over the world to live there. As transport and communication improved in the last century, more and more people moved to cities far away to find work or family members. The influx of foreigners and their traditions is what makes cities so vibrant and fascinating.

MURALS

Murals are drawings on walls. City murals, such as this one in Manchester, usually promote peace and the tolerance of others in a culturally diverse environment.

INTERNATIONAL SCHOOLS

Every big city has international schools for the children of the expatriated community. These children learn up to three or four languages from a very young age.

CHINA TOWN

Immigrants tend to come in waves and establish their quarters in the city. In New York, for instance, the Italian immigrants settled in "Little Italy" and the Chinese in "China Town".

AMAZING FACTS

★ More than 170 languages are spoken in New York City.

STREET PARADES

The colourful Notting Hill Carnival celebrates cultural diversity right in the heart of London. It is a way for people to share their cultural heritage with others.

Big crowds turn up *for the carnival, which attracts tourists from all over the world*

A young girl proudly *wears her national flag as a headscarf*

The band *keeps the rhythm as people dance*

Children wear *brightly coloured dresses and make-up*

CONNECTING PEOPLE

Many cities in Europe are now connected by high-speed trains, allowing people to travel like never before.

FIND OUT MORE
GREAT INVENTIONS: Skyscrapers
TRANSPORT: Cars

Mainland Southeast Asia

The countries in mainland Southeast Asia are Myanmar, Thailand, Laos, Vietnam, Cambodia, Malaysia and Singapore. The people in these countries govern, or rule, their countries in different ways and speak many different languages. But they also share many customs and religions. Many Malaysian people are Muslims and follow the religion of Islam, but most people in this region are Buddhists.

A MONK'S LIFE
Many young boys from Buddhist families leave home when they are about eight years old to study to be monks. Their hair is shaved off, and they spend their time praying and studying the teachings of Buddha, a religious leader who lived hundreds of years ago.

Novices, or trainee monks, study Buddha's life and teachings

RICE AND LOTUS BLOSSOM
A boy who is studying to be a monk is not allowed to work and must beg for his food. He carries a begging bowl and waits for people to fill it. He burns incense, and leaves rice and sacred lotus blossoms in temples, as a kind of prayer.

Studying to be a monk in a monastery school in Thailand

Begging *bowl*

Rice

Incense sticks

Lotus blossom

Temple offering

Incense burner

RAINY DAYS
The countries of Southeast Asia have monsoons, when it rains heavily for weeks. Roads have special drains, but they still often flood. Children must sometimes wade to and from school.

Children playing on the water-filled streets of Phnom Penh, Vietnam

Floating market at Inle Lake, Myanmar

KEEPING AFLOAT
Each morning, traders who live near rivers or lakes fill their boats with fruit, spices and flowers. Shoppers paddle up to the boats or call them over to their homes built along the sides of the river.

Buddhist books are written in an ancient language called Pali

Durian

Mango

Pineapple

Paw-paw

Banana

Lychee

Fruit from Southeast Asia

AMAZING FACTS
★ A young Buddhist monk is allowed only one meal a day, and it must be eaten before noon.

★ The Thai name for Bangkok is Krung Thep, which means "City of Angels."

FIND OUT MORE
ATLAS OF THE WORLD: Asia
THE WORLD OF ART: Buddhist art

Maritime Southeast Asia

The countries of Indonesia, the Philippines, Brunei and Papua New Guinea form groups of thousands of islands stretching into the Pacific and Indian Oceans. Many people live in small fishing or farming villages. Many others live and work in large, crowded cities, such as Manila in the Philippines and Jakarta in Indonesia.

FISHING VILLAGE

The Philippines is made up of over 7,000 islands, and thousands of tiny fishing villages line the coasts. The villagers set out nearly every day to fish on the coral reefs and the open sea beyond. Children help their parents catch and clean fish before and after school.

Houses often have *one long room inside*

Roofs are made *of palm leaves*

Fishing village on Panay Island, the Philippines

Fishing nets *are tied to long wooden poles*

Wooden stilts help to protect *houses from monsoon floods and high tides*

DRIVING A JEEPNEY

On the crowded streets of Manila, thousands of people travel by jeepney. These buses were once army jeeps, but have been changed to carry passengers. Most jeepneys are painted in bright colours and are decorated with mirrors, horns and tassels.

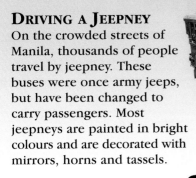

Brightly-coloured jeepney

LAND OF LANGUAGES

Papua New Guinea has over 800 different languages. Sometimes, people from different villages can talk to each other only through a translator, who tells each person what the other is saying. In schools, children learn the country's national language of English.

Schoolchildren in Jonba, Madang, Papua New Guinea

SARONGS AND SNEAKERS

People in Southeast Asia wear loose clothing, such as sarongs, because of the heat. A sarong is a piece of cloth, wrapped loosely around the waist like a skirt. At home, many children like to wear a combination of traditional sarongs with T-shirts and sneakers, or training shoes.

Sarong made from batik –
a process that uses wax and dye to make patterns on cloth

Children wearing sarongs

AMAZING FACTS

★ Indonesia is made up of nearly 14,000 islands.

★ Brunei is one of the smallest countries in the world, but its ruler, the Sultan, is one of the world's richest men because his country has lots of oil.

FIND OUT MORE
ATLAS OF THE WORLD: Asia
COMMUNICATIONS: Language

India and its Neighbours

Huge billboards show scenes from the latest Indian movies

There are over 900 million people living in India, and millions of others live in the countries near it – Pakistan, Bangladesh, Nepal, Bhutan and Sri Lanka. Many people in this area have moved from the countryside to find work in large cities. Factories make modern goods such as computers and televisions, but people in villages still use old ways of farming.

Elephants are decorated with colourful cloth hangings and strings of lights

City streets are crowded with traffic and people

Making a movie on the streets of Bombay

Buddhist festival of Esala Perahera

ELEPHANT FESTIVAL

The Esala Perahera Buddhist festival is held in Kandy, Sri Lanka, every July. The streets are full of dancers, acrobats, flame throwers and nearly 100 elephants.

AMAZING FACTS

★ In some Indian villages there are nearly as many cows as people. This is because most Indian people are Hindus, and they believe that cows are holy so they do not eat them.

24

LIGHTS! CAMERA! ACTION!

India produces around 800 movies each year, more than any other country in the world. Most movies are filmed in studios in Bombay, although some scenes are filmed on the city's streets. The Indian movie industry is called Bollywood.

HENNAED HANDS

Young women in India use a red dye to decorate their hands and feet for weddings and festivals. The dye is made by mixing henna leaves with oil and grinding them into a paste.

Detailed patterns take many hours to paint

Lighting

SCHOOL'S OUT!

In Pakistan, boys and girls are usually taught separately, at different schools. In villages, however, children are often taught together and classes may be held outside.

School children in an outdoor class in a village in northern Pakistan

Camera crew

The director *makes sure that everything and everyone is in place before filming*

FIND OUT MORE
ATLAS OF THE WORLD: India
GREAT INVENTIONS: Movies

Central and Southwest Asia

☞ This area includes the countries in the centre and southwest of Asia, from Afghanistan and Kazakhstan to Saudi Arabia and part of Turkey. Much of this area is dry desert or grassland, and many children and their families herd sheep or goats. Most people in this region are Muslims, but the area also includes the Jewish nation of Israel.

Cold yogurt drinks wash down the meal

Mealtime in a traditional home in Saudi Arabia

FAMILY MEAL

In traditional Arab families throughout southwest Asia, men and women usually eat separately. At mealtime, people sit on the floor, with the food laid out on a rug in front of them.

Loose white robe keeps the wearer cool

Tents made of woven goat hair

LIVING IN TENTS

The Bedouins are a group of nomadic, or travelling, people living in countries such as Oman. Today, many Bedouins live in towns and villages, but for part of the year they wander across the desert, living in portable tents.

For Bedouins, camels are still a sign of wealth

Bedouins camping in the desert

Young children in a kibbutz kindergarten

In traditional Arab families, people eat with their right hand

Shurba is a soup made from yogurt, rice, onions and pasta

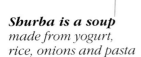

KIBBUTZ KIDS
Some children in Israel live in kibbutzim, which are villages built around a farm or factory. Kibbutzim were set up by Jewish families so that they could live together and share the work and produce. Older children often help on the kibbutzim during the day, when they are not at school.

FESTIVAL FOOD
Muslim people follow the religion of Islam. Like people of other religions, they have special foods to celebrate religious festivals. *Ma'moul* are small cookies made by mixing semolina, dates and pistachio nuts.

Ma'moul may be eaten during the festival of Eid

FIND OUT MORE
ATLAS OF THE WORLD: Asia
FROM STONE AGE TO SPACE AGE: Muslims

Living in the Countryside

In many countries, children live in villages in the countryside, far from the nearest city or even town. Many of these children live on farms and help their parents with some of the farm work.

Most children who live on farms have small jobs to do before school or when they come home. These jobs help their parents and also help the children learn more about the farm. They may gather firewood, fetch water, herd animals or collect eggs. Most children who live on farms still have time to go to school and play games like other children.

KENYAN VILLAGE LIFE

The Maasais live in villages in Kenya and help each other as if they were part of a team. Each tribe makes recognisable huts. When they are not in school the children sometimes gather wood or collect water from the well to help their parents.

Many young *in the commu* *become shephe*

Women use a *large wooden mortar to pound millet for food preparations*

Collecting eggs on a farm in France

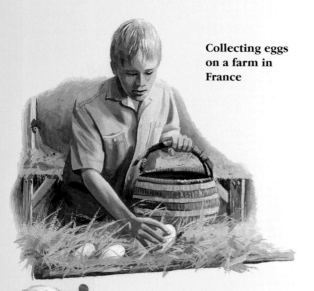

Huts are made *of mud and reed, and rooftops can be covered with palm leaves or a mix of mud and grass*

Children help *their mother to draw water from the well*

GETTING TO SCHOOL

In many countries, the local school might be several kilometres from a village. Children must walk or cycle to school if there is no bus or train to take them.

Cycling to school in Java, Indonesia

TRAVELLING DOCTOR

Many village children live in areas that are far from the nearest doctor's surgery or hospital. In many countries, travelling doctors visit villages to treat sick people and give injections to keep children healthy.

Travelling doctor in Nigeria, Africa

FIND OUT MORE
ATLAS OF THE WORLD: Africa
FROM STONE AGE TO SPACE AGE: The First Farmers

29

Russia

Russia covers more land than any other country in the world. It stretches from Western Europe right across Asia to the Pacific Ocean in the east. The far north of the country is frozen with ice, and few people live there. Most children and their families live in small apartments in towns and cities in the western part of the country. Russia has warm summers, but its winters are bitterly cold.

BALLET SCHOOL

Ballet is the most popular type of dance in Russia. The best young dancers go to ballet schools where they practice hard. They hope that one day they will dance with a famous ballet troupe.

Coppelia performed by the Bolshoi Ballet

The barre is a long railing *that the dancers hold for balance when practicing*

The ballet teacher *teaches the graceful positions and movements*

Male *dancers wear long tights*

Female dancers, called *ballerinas, wear one-piece leotards and ballet shoes*

Ballet shoes have *hard tips to help dancers stand on their toes*

A NEST OF RUSSIAN DOLLS

The two halves of a colourful Russian doll called a *matrioshka* can be pulled apart to reveal another smaller doll inside. When that one is divided there is yet another doll, and so on. Children love to take apart the *matrioshka* and put them back together.

AMAZING FACTS

★ Russia is so big it takes eight days to cross it by train from Moscow to Vladivostok.

Ballerinas wear long hair tied up in a topknot

The thick wool of a sheepskin hat also keeps out rain

Soured cream   *Tea and jam*

Blini

Russian tea

SHEEPSKIN HAT

Sheep are raised in the Russian mountains, and people use the wool to make most of their clothes. Some people wear a thick sheepskin hat all year. It is warm in winter, but keeps the head cool in the hot summer.

BLINI AND TEA

Blini are thin pancakes, often served with soured cream and fillings. Many Russians eat blini with tea, which they drink from a glass. They sweeten the tea with a spoonful of jam.

Ballet class in Moscow, Russia

FIND OUT MORE
ATLAS OF THE WORLD: Russia
DANCE, DRAMA AND MUSIC: Ballet

Eastern Europe

The region called Eastern Europe includes the countries just to the west of Russia, as well as Poland, the Czech Republic, Slovakia, Hungary, Romania and Bulgaria. These countries have a varied mix of people with different customs and ways of life, including the Serbians, Croatians and the Romany people.

LIVING ON A FARM

Farming is important in Eastern Europe, even though these countries have many factories. Most farms are small, and families grow potatoes, wheat and other vegetables. Farmers have used some of the same ways of planting and harvesting for hundreds of years.

Most farms have a small barn where farmers store grain or keep animals

Children help out on the farm before and after school

Traditional farm in Hungary

Wooden roof has steep sides so winter snow slides off

Chickens and other poultry roam freely on the farm

AMAZING FACTS

★ In Bulgaria, a shake of the head from left to right means "yes" and a nod means "no."

★ Transylvania in Romania has a rich folk history. Stories of the vampire Dracula are based on Vlad the Impaler, a cruel prince who lived there in the 1400s.

TRADITIONAL DANCES

Eastern Europe is famous for its folk dances, which began as part of village harvest celebrations and at other times in the farming year. Children learn dances such as the polka and the mazurka. They often wear traditional costumes when they dance.

Traditional folk dance from Latvia

Boy watering plants in a window box

WINDOW GARDENS

Polish people love flowers, and even people who live in city apartments grow flowers in window boxes. Over half of all Polish families live in apartments because many houses were destroyed during World War II. Apartment buildings are everywhere, even in the countryside.

CHILDREN'S MOVIES

Many Czech movies are based on children's folk tales. Most use real actors, but the films of Jan Švankmajer and other directors are either cartoons or they feature lifelike puppets.

Scene from the film *Alice* by Jan Švankmajer

FIND OUT MORE
ATLAS OF THE WORLD: Europe
COMMUNICATIONS: Cartoons

Western Europe

The countries of Western Europe are some of the most crowded in the world. Most people live in cities or towns where there are many factories and other places of work. Most of these countries have joined together to form the European Union, which allows businesses in each country to trade with one another more easily.

CITY SQUARE
Many European cities are very old. Most have large squares, which are the traditional meeting points in each city. Cafés and restaurants line these squares, where people can relax over a drink or a meal.

Awnings *provide shade when the sun is hot*

RIVER LIFE
Long, narrow barges carry goods along Europe's large rivers, such as the River Rhine, which flows through Germany and the Netherlands. Some of these barges are family homes. Children play on the decks among potted plants and lines of drying washing.

Children on a barge on the Rhine, in the Netherlands

City square in Paris, France

BY THE MEDITERRANEAN
An older, slower way of life continues in some parts of Western Europe. In small fishing villages around the Mediterranean Sea, people mend fishing nets before having a siesta, or short sleep, in the hot afternoon.

Fishing village near Naples, Italy

Graceful archways *rise over the entrance to many city squares*

Puppet shows, mime *performances and acrobatics are popular street entertainments*

Cooling fountains *are found in many squares*

FOOD FOR A FEAST

Some of the most popular foods in the world come from Europe. Tasty food includes Italian pasta and pizza, spicy sausages from Germany, cheeses from France and French fries – which were actually invented in Belgium.

French fries

Spaghetti (a kind of pasta) with bolognese sauce

Pizza

AMAZING FACTS

★ Europe is the world's second-smallest continent, but it has more people living in it than North America, which is nearly two and a half times bigger.

FIND OUT MORE
ATLAS OF THE WORLD: Europe
GREAT TRAVELLERS AND EXPLORERS: Pizza

Scandinavia

☞The countries of Scandinavia – Norway, Sweden, Denmark and Finland – are at the northern edge of Europe. Iceland, an island country in the Atlantic Ocean, is also part of Scandinavia. Here, winters are long, cold and dark. In winter in northern Scandinavia, the Sun does not rise for several months. In summer, it does not set. Scandinavia is sometimes called the Land of the Midnight Sun.

Goggles or sunglasses protect the eyes from sunlight reflecting off the snow

In Iceland, families can swim outside in hot springs, even during the cold, snowy winter

CROSS-COUNTRY SKIING

Cross-country skiing is a popular winter sport in Scandinavia. It was invented in Norway many years ago as a good way of getting around in the snow. Children in many villages ski to school.

GUSHING GEYSERS

Iceland has many geysers, or springs, where hot water gushes from under the ground. The hot water is used to warm the water of swimming pools and even to heat homes.

Children skiing to school

Children wear *padded jackets and pants, and thick hats to keep warm*

Houses in the *country are built from local timber, or wood*

LAPP FARMERS

The Lapp people, also known as the Saami, once wandered across northern Finland into Russia, herding reindeer. Today, many Lapps are settling in towns and villages in Finland.

Preparing sleds for a reindeer race in Lapland

CITY DWELLERS

Most Scandinavian children live in towns or large cities such as Copenhagen in Denmark, Oslo in Norway, Stockholm in Sweden and Helsinki in Finland. These capital cities are all by the sea. In winter, the sea in their harbours often freezes over.

Summer in Copenhagen harbour, Denmark

Skiers use poles to *keep their balance and to push them forward*

Short cross-country, *or Nordic, skis*

AMAZING FACTS

★ Most children living in Scandinavia are already good skiers by the time they are old enough to go to school.

Heels lift free, *with each stride*

FIND OUT MORE
ATLAS OF THE WORLD: Scandinavia
PLANET EARTH: Geysers

Games and Pastimes

Children all over the world love playing games. Nearly every child has played "chase" or hide-and-seek. Games played in different countries are often similar but have different names.

Pastimes, or hobbies, are also popular. They include making or collecting different kinds of objects. Sports are games involving physical exercise. Some sports, such as baseball, cricket and football, are played in teams. In others, such as "singles" tennis, people play by themselves against one other person, or opponent.

Clapping games, with special songs or rhymes, are played in nearly every schoolground

FOOTBALL CRAZY

Football is played in almost every country in the world and is the world's most popular sport. Children set up goal-posts and play on the beach or in a park. Many hope that one day they will be good enough to play for their country's football team.

Children learn to control the ball on fine sand

COMPUTER GAMES

Computer games are played on home computers or on small handheld sets. Games are usually played by one person, who tries to improve his or her score each time. Most computer games are made in Japan.

Computer games are usually expensive compared with other games and toys

Children playing snakes and ladders

IT'S YOUR MOVE

Board games are popular with children in many countries. Some games, such as the Japanese game *go*, are played only in the country in which they were invented. Others, such as checkers and snakes and ladders, are known nearly everywhere.

Football ball

MAKING MODELS

A lot of children like to make models. Some models come in kits, with instructions on how to make them. But some children use their imagination to make models from cardboard, sticks, stones, or other things they find.

African boy with a model truck made out of wire and bottle tops

Pile of clothes *makes up each goalpost*

The goalkeeper *tries to stop players from the other team scoring a goal*

Boys and girls playing football on a beach in Brazil

FIND OUT MORE
COMMUNICATIONS: Computers
SPORT: Football

39

North and West Africa

☞**M**any North African countries, such as Morocco and Algeria, border the great Sahara Desert. Children avoid the hot sun by staying in the shade and wearing loose clothing. Nigeria, Ghana and other countries south of the Sahara are also hot, but they have many forests and heavy rains. A school day stops if the sound of the rain makes it too noisy to hear the teacher.

Covered streets are shady and cool

DESERT WANDERERS

The Tuareg nomadic people live along the edges of the Sahara Desert. Families travel from oasis to oasis, where there is water for their cattle. Children soon learn to ride camels – the best way of getting around on the hot sand.

Shops are open to the street so that buyers can see what is for sale

Donkeys carry heavy loads to and from the souk

Cloth veil keeps sand away from the rider's face

Souk in Tunis, the capital of Tunisia

Boy wears traditional dark blue robes of the Tuareg people

Boy riding camel in desert

SHOPPING IN THE SOUK

Many towns in North Africa have busy souks, or markets. In narrow, crowded passages, people can buy fruit, meat, carpets and clothes. Children learn from their parents how to bargain to get the best price.

40

GROWING TOWNS

Towns and cities in this region are growing very fast as families move from the countryside to find work. Many towns have grown up by the sea or along rivers and people often travel by boat.

People living in a shanty town by a busy new road outside Lagos, Nigeria

Finely woven rugs are made of wool

Shoppers drink tea while they choose what to buy

DRUM TALK

People in forest villages throughout northern and western Africa use drums as a way of sending messages. Children know the special beats that mean "mealtime," "celebrations," or "danger."

AMAZING FACTS

★ The traditional drink in Morocco is mint tea, served with lots of sugar and a sprig of mint. It is offered free of charge to customers before they begin to bargain for what they want to buy.

FIND OUT MORE
ATLAS OF THE WORLD: Africa
PLANET EARTH: Deserts

Central and Southern Africa

☞There are many countries in central and southern Africa with different kinds of land and climate. Some, like Congo, contain thick rain forests where children travel by canoe along the rivers. Others, such as Zimbabwe and Tanzania, have open grasslands where children help their parents to herd cattle. Other children live in big cities, such as Pretoria in South Africa or Harare in Zimbabwe.

ZULU DANCE

The Zulus are the largest group of tribespeople in southern Africa. Many Zulu people are now farmers, but for celebrations they dress in warrior clothes and perform traditional dances. Like other tribes, the Zulus are trying to keep their ancient ways of life alive. Older people teach children the stories and dances that tell of Zulu history.

Dramatic
headdresses are
made of feathers

Zulu shields
are made from
the skin of an ox

Dancers carry
walking sticks
called knobkerries

Zulu dancers

Leg ties are
made from
a lion's mane

LIANA WALK

Some children living in central Africa never see a road or a railroad. Thick forests and roaring rivers cut off their farms from cities and towns. Boys and girls must cross shaky bridges made of liana vines to visit people in other villages.

Children on a liana bridge

A group of mixed races in South Africa

END OF APARTHEID

For many years, South Africa had laws that separated people of different races. The laws, known as *apartheid*, began to change in 1990. South African children are now allowed to live and play together.

ON THE RIGHT TRACK

Some of the best runners in the world come from southern Africa. Many children from small villages run long distances to and from school each day, so they are used to running from an early age.

Running a friendly race on an African beach

AMAZING FACTS

★ On the island of Madagascar a man must make a speech before he is married. If the speech is no good, he pays a fine and starts again.

★ Lake Malawi covers one-quarter of the country of Malawi. Fish from the lake provide people's main source of food.

FIND OUT MORE
ATLAS OF THE WORLD: Africa
FAMOUS PEOPLE: Nelson Mandela

South America

The high Andes Mountains run down the western side of South America, through Colombia, Ecuador, Peru, Bolivia and Chile. Life in the mountains can be hard. People wear hats and thick woolen clothing to keep warm. Some of the countries to the east of the Andes Mountains have hot, wet jungles. These thick rain forests cover most of Brazil, its northern neighbours and parts of Peru, Bolivia and Paraguay.

MOUNTAIN MARKET

Market days in the Andes attract buyers and sellers from all around. Women come from farms with loads of potatoes, onions, oats and other crops. Some women walk many kilometres through the mountains to reach the market.

Women wear a piece of cloth, called an ahuayo, *as a wrap and to carry heavy loads*

Goods are spread out on the ground in front of the traders

Market day in the Andes

Children line up for school in San Ignacio, Peru

MOUNTAIN SCHOOL

Classes in many schools in the mountain countries of South America are held in Spanish. However, teachers often speak to the children in Quechua or Aymara, which are both Native American languages.

AMAZING FACTS

★ La Paz, the capital of Bolivia, is the world's highest capital city. It is 4,100 m (13,450 ft) above sea level – so high up that the air is very thin and visitors often find it difficult to breathe.

Fishing on the banks of the Amazon River in Brazil

ON THE RIVER BANK

Many Native South Americans, such as the Yanomami tribe of Brazil, still live in tiny villages in the remote rain forests. Children wash and swim in the river, but they must watch out for alligators, snakes and vicious piranha fish.

Carnival parade in Rio de Janeiro

CARNIVAL TIME!

Children love carnival time – an exciting celebration that takes place each year at the start of the Christian festival of Lent. The biggest carnival is held in Rio de Janeiro. Thousands of people dress in fancy costumes and spend the day dancing in the streets.

The derby is a type of hat popular among the women of the high Andes

FIND OUT MORE
ATLAS OF THE WORLD: South America
REPTILES AND AMPHIBIANS: Alligators

Mexico, Central America and the Caribbean

Central America is the name given to the eight countries that link North America and South America. The largest of these countries is Mexico. To the east is a long chain of beautiful islands in the Caribbean Sea. This region has a wide variety of ethnic groups, or people of different races, such as Asian, Afro-Caribbean, Arawak and European.

DAY OF THE DEAD

Each November 1, Mexicans celebrate the Day of the Dead. In the festival, families burn candles by the graves of their relatives. They believe their relatives will return to Earth for just one night. It is a happy time, when everyone remembers people they have loved.

Market traders sell flowers, tiny figures made of paper or candy, and banners to decorate homes and graves

Children decorate candy skulls with their name

AMAZING FACTS

★ Mexico City is the largest city in the world. More than 20 million people live there and it is still growing.

Chocolate skulls and other candies are eaten by children as a treat

Buying candy and flowers at a market stall in Mexico to celebrate the Day of the Dead

Caribbean children playing steel drums

STEEL BAND

The people of Trinidad and other Caribbean islands love the music of steel bands. Children learn to strike notes on old steel barrels that have been made into musical instruments. Steel bands are also popular with the many tourists who spend their vacations in the Caribbean.

Paper banners with pictures of ghosts and goblins

Colourful flowers, such as orange marigolds, are sold to welcome back the dead

SCHOOL GARDENS

Children in Cuba learn about farming by growing crops and herbs in special gardens at their schools. Everyone has a turn at digging, planting and harvesting the crops. Some of the plants harvested by the children are later used to make medicines.

Cuban children in their school garden

FIND OUT MORE
ATLAS OF THE WORLD: Mexico
DANCE, DRAMA AND MUSIC: Percussion

Celebrations and Festivals

Children all over the world look forward to celebrations and festivals that take place through the year. Some festivals, such as the Day of the Dead in Mexico, are special to one particular country. Others, such as New Year, are celebrated by people in many different countries.

Many celebrations are linked to religions – for example, the Christian festival of Christmas and the Hindu festival of Diwali. Others are seasonal – the Japanese celebrate the cherry blossoms in the spring, and the Russians celebrate the first winter snow.

MAYPOLE DANCING

Some children in northern Europe welcome spring by dancing around a maypole. They usually wear colourful costumes, and girls put garlands of flowers in their hair. One girl is chosen to lead the celebrations as the May Queen.

The maypole is made from the wood of a tall, straight tree such as a fir tree

Dancers weave around the maypole holding colourful ribbons which become wrapped around the pole

Bright clothes are worn to celebrate the arrival of spring flowers and longer, lighter days

Maypole festival in the United Kingdom

Musician playing a cello

Star lantern

Masks for sale
*at stalls look
like the moon
or animals*

**Trung Thu lantern
festival in Vietnam**

BIRTHDAY CAKES

Every year, many children celebrate the day on which they were born – their birthday. Some children have a birthday cake with candles on it, one for every year of their life. Friends join in the party and bring presents.

**Blowing out
candles on a
birthday cake**

LANTERN FESTIVAL

Children in many Asian countries join in a lantern festival each fall at the time of the full Moon. They walk through the streets with glowing lanterns. Stalls sell special sweet moon cakes during the celebration.

PINATA PARTY

At Mexican parties, children try to smash a colourful papier-mâché model called a piñata. They take turns to be blindfolded and then swing a bat at the piñata, which hangs from a rope. Candy comes showering down when the piñata breaks.

**Girl trying to
break the piñata**

FIND OUT MORE
THE WORLD OF ART: Papier mâché
GREAT TRAVELLERS AND EXPLORERS:
Festivals

The United States of America

The United States of America has a wide mixture of people, customs and traditions. This is because people from different countries have moved there over the last 400 years. These people have settled in their new country and have made it their home. About three-quarters of Americans live in towns and cities.

Lantern made from a hollowed-out pumpkin

THANKSGIVING

Americans celebrate Thanksgiving Day each November by sitting down to a big family feast. The tradition of Thanksgiving began in 1621, when some of the first English settlers gave thanks to God for a good harvest.

Most families celebrate Thanksgiving, whether they were originally from Italy, Mexico, Greece, Africa, England or China

At Thanksgiving, families usually set the table with their best dishes and glasses

AMAZING FACTS

★ At the very first Thanksgiving meal in 1621, the main dish was not turkey, but eels.

★ Four out of every five Americans speak English. The second most spoken language is Spanish.

Family enjoying Thanksgiving dinner

Pumpkins are mashed and sweetened to make tasty pies

Cranberry sauce has a tangy taste that goes well with turkey

Roast turkey fills the house with a delicious smell

TRICK OR TREAT?

October 31 is Halloween, an ancient festival when ghosts were thought to return to Earth. At Halloween, children love to dress in scary costumes. They go from house to house and threaten to play tricks if they do not get a treat such as candy.

Children dressed up for Halloween

Some relatives *travel long distances to join their family*

Enjoying a film at the Sony Imax movie theatre in New York City

SPECIAL EFFECTS

Movies seem almost like real life at some movie theatres in New York. Children wear special headsets that make the movie images appear to leap off the screen toward them.

Children swear the Pledge of Allegiance – promising to be loyal to their country

FLYING THE FLAG

The American flag has 50 stars – one for every state in the union. Americans feel their flag is a symbol of how the country is united. At the beginning of the school day, children stand with their hands on their hearts and promise to be loyal to the flag and their country.

FIND OUT MORE
ATLAS OF THE WORLD: United States
COMMUNICATIONS: Flags

Canada

People from many nations have helped Canada grow. The first European settlers came from Britain and France. Today, Canada has two official languages – English and French. The Inuit people of the far north and the other Native Americans have lived in Canada for more than 10,000 years. Canada shares many customs with its southern neighbor, the United States.

TRAVELLING BY SKI-DOO

A ski-doo, or snowmobile, is like a motorcycle with tracks and skis instead of wheels. In the far north of Canada it is snowy for most of the year. People use ski-doos to help them get around more easily. Ski-doos are much faster than using dogs to pull a sled – the traditional way of travelling.

Snowplows help clear the snow from roads

The guard wears bright clothes so he can easily be seen by the traffic

SNOWY SCHOOL DAYS

Many places in Canada have long, snowy winters. Children must be very careful walking through the snow because drivers cannot see them easily.

STOP

SCHOOL GUARD

Going to school in a blizzard

A crossing guard stops traffic to let children cross the street to school

Cars have chains on their tires to give them more grip in slippery snow

Inuit family on a snowmobile outside a store in Hudson Bay

GUARDIAN ANGELS

The Native Americans of western Canada carved huge totem poles out of trees. The poles told family histories and guarded the doorways to homes.

Carved animals

Native American totem pole

SWEET SYRUP

Maple syrup comes from sugar maple trees. Maple sap is collected from the trees then boiled until it thickens into syrup. Maple syrup is often used on pancakes or bread. Pouring hot syrup into the snow turns it into maple taffy, a type of candy.

Children wear *several layers of* *clothing to keep* *warm*

Children making fresh maple taffy

AMAZING FACTS

★ In winter, some people flood their back gardens with water so that it freezes to make a temporary ice rink for skating or ice hockey.

FIND OUT MORE

ATLAS OF THE WORLD: Canada
THE WORLD OF ART: Totem poles

Australasia

Australasia is the name given to Australia, New Zealand and many small islands in the Pacific Ocean. Australia is a huge country. Many people have come to live in Australia since the first Europeans settled there about 200 years ago. The Aboriginal people have lived there much longer – perhaps as long as 40,000 years. New Zealand is smaller than Australia. It has many farms and a few large cities.

LIVING BY THE SEA

Most big Australian cities, such as Sydney, have grown up along the coast. This is because it is cooler than the Outback, the name given to the hot desert areas in the centre of the country.

The roof of Sydney Opera House looks like the sails of a boat

AMAZING FACTS

★ Sheep farming is important in New Zealand. The country has about 50 million sheep – that's over 16 times more sheep than people.

Children living in Australia often have ancestors or parents who originally came from England, Italy, Greece, China, or Vietnam

Many families in Australia enjoy the outdoor life

Children playing on a trampoline on an Aboriginal reserve

ABORIGINAL COMMUNITIES

Most Aborigines live in large cities but Aboriginal land councils across Australia help preserve Aboriginal languages, culture and ways of life. Aboriginal people work hard to keep their special closeness to the land.

Sydney Harbor Bridge and Opera House are famous Australian landmarks

Windsurfing is a popular sport on most Australian beaches

Children hiking in the New Zealand mountains

Suncream protects people from the hot sun

MAORI LIFE

The Maoris were the first settlers of New Zealand. They came from the Polynesian Islands of the Pacific Ocean about 1,200 years ago. Maori tribes are like huge families. Grandparents teach children stories in the Maori language.

Children learning about Maori history

ROOM TO ROAM

New Zealand is as big as the United Kingdom, yet it only has about 3 million people. The country has two main islands – North Island and South Island. Three-quarters of the population live on North Island, where the climate is warmer. Many New Zealanders like to hike through their country's beautiful forests and mountains. Older children often camp overnight.

FIND OUT MORE
ATLAS OF THE WORLD: Australasia
FROM STONE AGE TO SPACE AGE:
Australian Aborigines

Glossary of Key Words

Ancestor: A member of a person's family, or race, who lived many generations before them.

Buddhist: A person who follows the teachings of Buddha, a religious leader who lived about seven centuries ago.

Carnival: A celebration that includes merrymaking, dancing and parades. It sometimes marks the start of the Christian festival of Lent, which leads up to Easter.

Celebration: A special holiday or event, usually held at the same time each year.

Christian: A person who believes that Jesus Christ is the son of God.

Climate: The usual pattern of weather in an area over a long time.

Continent: One of the seven large land masses into which the Earth's land is divided. The seven continents are Asia, Australia, North America, South America, Europe, Africa and Antarctica.

Costume: The special style or way of dressing of a particular nation. Many countries have traditional or historical costume that is worn at festivals or at important events.

Country: An area with exact geographical boundaries where the people usually share a language and a set of traditions.

Custom: A way of behaving that a particular group of people has had for a long time.

Earthquake: A shaking of the ground caused by a sudden release of energy stored in the rocks under the Earth's surface.

Ethnic group: A group of people who share the same language, traditions and, often, the same religion.

Factory: A building or workshop with machinery or equipment that is used to manufacture, or make, goods.

Festival: A particular day or days that celebrate an event or that mark an important time of year.

Harvesting: The gathering of crops when they are ripe.

Hindu: A person who follows Hinduism, a religion based on sacred writings from Ancient India.

Incense: A substance used in religious ceremonies that smells sweet when it is burnt.

Jewish: Following the religion of Judaism. The holy book of Jewish people, or Jews, is the Jewish Bible. Christians know it as the Old Testament.

Language: The way in which people use words to talk to each other or to write things down.

Maritime: Relating to the sea.

Monk: A man who devotes his life to a religion and who belongs to a religious community.

Monsoon: A summer wind that blows from the Indian Ocean into Southeast Asia. It brings heavy rain from May to September.

Museum: A building that houses and displays items of great value and historic interest.

Muslim: A person who follows Islam, a religion based on the words of God as spoken to the Prophet Muhammad.

Nationality: The state of belonging to a particular nation, where people usually share the same language and history.

Nomad: A person who wanders from place to place, and who has no fixed home.

Oasis: An area in a desert around a well or spring. There is usually enough water to support plants.

Polluted: Damaged or made dirty by waste materials, such as smoke, fumes or garbage.

Population: The number of people living in a certain place.

Race: A group of people who share the same ancestors.

Religion: A group of beliefs that tries to explain all things and that usually accepts that there is a god or gods controlling all life.

Seasonal: Happening at a particular time of year, or season, such as spring or winter.

Shanty town: A poor and often badly built part of a town.

State: A group of people organised as a political community under one government.

Temple: A building for religious worship, believed to be the Earthly home of a god or goddess.

Trader: A person who buys and sells things, especially in a market.

Tradition: An idea or belief handed down from parents to their children over many years.

Translator: A person who can express the ideas of one language in a different language.

Tribe: A group of people descended from the same ancestors, and often with the same leader.

Troupe: A group of actors, dancers or singers.

Index

Acknowledgments

AUTHOR
Sean Connoly

CONSULTANT FOR CHILDREN OF THE WORLD
Dr Margaret Byron is a lecturer, tutor and examiner in the
Geography Department at King's College in London, England.
She specialises in human geography, issues concerning
developing and third world countries, and the Afro-Caribbean
culture in particular.

EDUCATIONAL CONSULTANTS
Lois Eskin, BSc, is a publishing consultant with special expertise
in organisational planning, research and product planning for
educational publishers.

Kurt W. Fischer, PhD, Professor at Harvard University,
Graduate School of Education.

INTERNATIONAL CONSULTANTS
Pamela Katherina Decho, BA (Hons), is a consultant editor
specialising in Latin America.

Zahara Wan is a consultant editor specialising in Southeast Asia.

Minghua Zhao, PhD, MSc, MA, BA, is a consultant editor
specialising in China and East Asia.

ILLUSTRATORS
Simone Boni, Joanne Cowne, Bill Donohoe, Pamela Goodchild,
Diane Fawcett, Kaye Hodges, Andre Hrydziusko, Biz Hull,
Michael Johnson, Nicki Palin, Helen Parsley, Roger Stewart,
Andrew Wheatcroft, Graham White, Joanna Williams,
Paul Wright. Disney art colouring: Neil Rigby.

FOR DISNEY ARTWORK IN THIS BOOK
Franco Valussi
With special thanks to Michael Horowitz and Carson Van Osten

AGENCY PHOTOGRAPHS
25 ZEFA; 27 Panos Pictures; 31 British Film Institute;
36 Tony Stone; 42 Sue Cunningham/SCP; 47b South American
Pictures; 51t Sony Imax; 52-53 B&C Alexander; 55 C F C L/Image
Select; 21b, 41b Tropix/M&V Birley; 16b Michael S Yamashita,
19l Francoise de Mulder, 21t Paul A Souders, 23t Barnabas
Bosshart, 28 Steve Raymer, 39 Daniel Laine, 43 Buddy Mays,
45b Kit Houghton and 47t Wolfgang Kaehler are from Corbis;
13 Jeff Greenberg, 34 Kim Hart and 23b, 35t & 45t are from
Robert Harding Picture Library; 16t, 19r, 35b, 41t and 51b
are from The Stock Market Picture Agency.

CHILDREN'S PHOTOGRAPHS
Ray Moller

PROJECT MANAGEMENT FOR DISNEY
With special thanks to Cally Chambers

PROJECT MANAGEMENT FOR PAPERVIEW
Isabelle Demolin, Delphine Prinselaar

COVER DESIGN
Louise Laurent

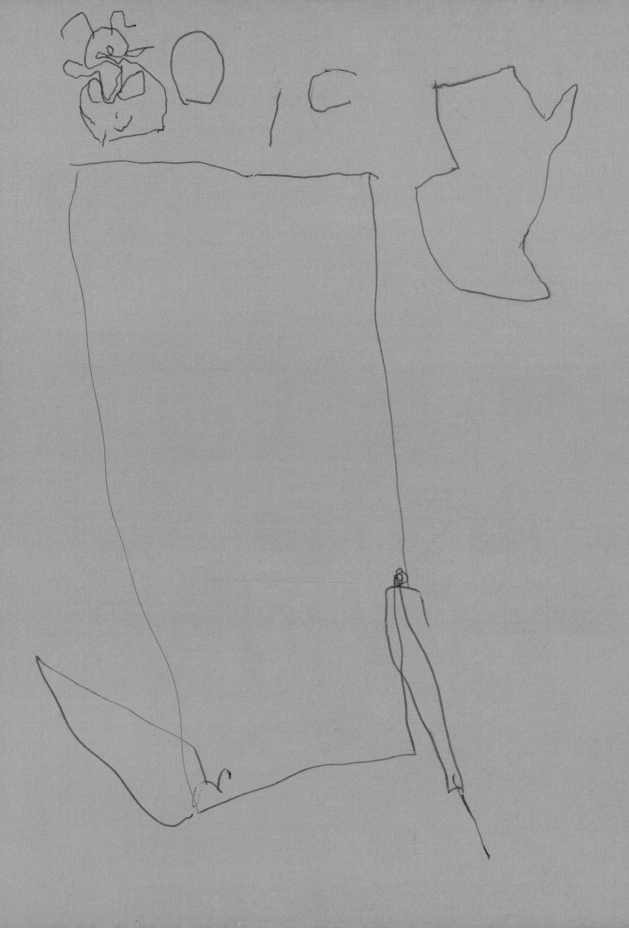